From the Heart of Me

Michael J Gardner AKA The Walking Poet

FIRST EDITION
Published in 2024 by
GREEN CAT BOOKS
19 St Christopher's Way
Pride Park
Derby
DE24 8JY
www.green-cat.shop

ISBN: 978-1-913794-80-4

CONTENTS

ACKNOWLEDGEMENTS

Thanks to the Brock's Hill Walking Group I lead each week for their support to me and their encouragement with my poetry.

From the Heart of Me

From the heart of me, out pours the passion.
It shapes the poetry I write with love and friendship, that is
my fashion.
I share the journey I've been through.
Dear reader, that within the words, you may feel the love and
friendship too.

If it is with a sense of loneliness or despair you live,
Seek a friend who from the heart of them, kindness and
compassion give.
And when in your life you have such a gift,
It relieves the loneliness, and your spirits' lift.

From the very heart of you,
Share the gift with others too.
And to them with kindness and compassion be a friend,
So the giving of that precious gift will never end.

A Child's Sadness

I see the sadness upon this child's face,
The tears that fall from the eyes and down his cheek, I trace.
They fall gently and bathe his feet,
As he, with hurt and heartache within himself doth meet.

Is it from the loss of a favourite book or toy
That brings tears and sadness to this young boy?
Or is it loss of brother, sister, father or mum
That the pain of grief doth come?

Let us, to him gather round,
And share the Christ-like love we've found,
That once again this young boy
Will know Christ's love, peace and joy.

Across a Grassy Meadow

I walk across a grassy meadow oh, so soft.
I see the birds glide and dive above the trees aloft.
The cattle race for feed across the ground
And make a loud thunder sound.

The stream gently flowing past,
Upon its banks, fishermen, their lines do cast,
Their catch they take home to their family,
And make a tasty dish for their tea.

And as I come to my country lane,
Back to my home again,
I stop and linger as on the garden gate I lean,
And reflect upon the treasure of all I've seen.

Adoration and Confession

Now it's time to sit and pray,
To express our love and confessions of our sins to say.
We speak with the Christ that we adore,
And seek forgiveness for our sins once more.

We place our life within his palm,
And seek forgiveness, peace and calm.
And as we pray, we seek His grace,
And hope to feel the love expressed upon his face.

Now as we come from speaking to Christ our Lord,
Now it's for Him to speak as we listen to His written word.
We take his message to our heart,
And seek to others, his message to impart.

<u>Advent is the Time</u>

Advent is the time to prepare,
Ready for when we see the Christ child, placed in that
manger there.
A time to prepare our hearts, so full of love and praise,
And pour it out to this special child upon whom we humbly
gaze.

A time to prepare the stable, and place the wise men and the
beasts;
Time to place the gold, frankincense and myrrh, and the gift
of love from your heart, a love that does not cease.

Time to prepare ourselves, ready to the stable go,
Once more to feel his love, and his promise of hope to know.

A Martian's Fear

The spaceship launches now for Mars,
Through the Milky Way, past planets and the stars.
The rocket leaves a vapour trail you could trace,
As off to its destination race.

The astronauts bounce and float around,
For there's no gravity with which to ground.
One said, "Do not worry, we'll be there soon,
Once we've passed that distant moon."

When they landed on Martian ground,
Down the gantry they did bound.
They looked across the terrain, both far and near,
Then suddenly a voice they hear.

"You can roam our planet as a friend,
But that is where our hospitality does end.
"Don't dig or mine our precious soil,
And our lovely planet spoil.
"What you've done to Earth brings shame,
Please, don't come here to do the same."

A Reminder to us All

As I walk to the shops on this new day,
I meet some friends along the way.
We walk into the Menphys Café.
We chat and drink and have a laugh.

Then we see the poster on the wall.
And it is a reminder to us all.
Their aim is to help each child you see,
Who suffers mental or physical disability.

So each time we sip our tea, whether strong or weak,
We help provide the support they seek.
So come with an open, caring heart
And bring new hope in a child's life to start.

A Ship's Return

A ship reveals itself from the mist,
As by the waves its bow is kissed.
The captain is aiming for the shore,
For his crew want to be back home once more.

The ship moors at the harbour side,
The crew rush down the gantry to their loved one's side.
Hugs and kisses all around
As they, once more their family found.

The terrors and trials of the sea
Are replaced by joy and much glee.
Glad to be back home with friends and family,
And share their love like you and me.

As I Gently Drift

As I drift gently on the cool waters of the stream,
I lay in comfort, taking time to dream.
And as I glide past the countryside,
My eyes, full of joyful amazement, are open wide.

I see the cattle lying peacefully on the ground,
Chewing the grass amidst the daisies all around.
And as I look up at the sky,
I see the birds go flying by.
A kingfisher dives to catch a fish,
And takes it home to share his tasty dish.

Now as I moor up along the bank,
I say a prayer, my Lord, to thank
For the beauty I have seen,
Oh, so quiet and serene.
The touch of God's hand I have felt,
Such a loving blessing doth cause my heart to melt.

A Weekly Chore

As I go down to the shops today,
I dodge the crowds as I make my way.
I hear the chatter of the crowd,
As they push and shove, and some shout so loud.

And so, I go into the store,
I pick up a basket so I can fill my fridge once more.
As I wander down each aisle,
I stop and linger awhile,
Trying to decide what to buy,
Tempted by that new line to try.

The basket that I had to fill,
I now take it full to the till.
The checkout lady scans each item one by one,
Then I scan my cash card when she's done.
This is just a weekly chore,
But I'll be back next week to do it once more.

The Candle of Peace

The candle of peace does not shine for today,
In the midst of conflict, the flame is blown away.
Let us, as brothers and sisters, our arms around them
embrace,
As in war, pain is what they now face.

Let us seek such wars to cease,
And help all nations dwell together in peace.
Let's pray for the candle of peace to shine once again,
And the nations be free from war, hurt and pain.

Down the Country Lane

As I walk down the country lane,
And feel the gentle summer rain.
In the field I see the rabbits bounding across the ground,
Being chased by a fox or possibly a hunting hound.

I feel the coolness of the breeze,
As it passes through the trees.
I hear the birds singing on each branch,
So beautiful it is, the sound puts my heart into a peaceful
trance.

As I walk along the riverside,
I see the swans as they, on the waters seem to glide.
The kingfisher dives and makes a splash,
Then shoots off with its catch at such a dash.

The starlings, a murmuration in the sky they make,
Each swirl, dip and dive so beautifully together take.
I've seen all this on my walk today,
And now in the silence a prayer of thanks, to God I say.

Friends

What a joy in life with friends to live,
Friends that kindness and compassion give.
Friends who, when help is needed, they are there for you,
And show their friendship to be true.

Friends who, when you're in grief or pain do cry,
Offer a shoulder and do not simply pass you by.
Friends who, through your labour give support and share your joy,
And enquire if it is a girl or boy.

Friends, who, when your life was dark and shattered,
That's when their friendship really mattered.
In that moment, friends gathered round to show their care without measure,
For friends truly are a precious treasure.

Friendship Like a Pearl

My friend, I am glad that you are here.
As we talk and walk, you help my loneliness disappear.
You share in fun and laughter, and kindness too.
This is the treasure that is you.

You help and say words of comfort when I shed a tear.
I'm glad I have a friend who shows kindness and comforts me
to ease my fear.

You came in my distress and darkest hour;
Into my life, you did kindness and compassion shower.
Our friendship I will always treasure,
it's a precious gift beyond all measure.

Our friendship, like a pearl, it dwells within my heart.
As I go through life, it's a treasure from which I never want
to part.

Harvest Meal

Together we share our harvest meal,
And within our heart the sense of Christian love and
friendship feel.
And as we sip the soup and break the bap,
And catch the crumbs upon our lap,
The thought of communion comes to mind,
And within my soul the joy of love and peace I find.

And as I continue to share with my friends,
I am praying that this kind fellowship never ends.
Thanks to those who prepared the meal,
Much gratitude to them I feel.
I pray in time there will be another,
So as God's children, we can share as sister and brother.

Ho, the Beauty

Ho, the beauty of the day,
As the sun doth rise to light our way.
Ho, the beauty of the sky,
And the birds as they fly by.
The trees, as they sway in the breeze,
Reveal the dappled beauty of their leaves.

The waters of the river flow,
And reflections of the sun doth show.
The mountains rise up so high,
They pierce the clouds that drift by.
The birds that dip and dive upon the wing,
Ho, the beauty of the song they sing.

Ho, this beauty I see each day,
As I journey on my way.
I treasure it with such glee
Because it really blesses me.
Now I go home and with friends, my journey share,
They tell me they wish they'd been there.

Hope

Whatever my troubles, whatever to me befall,
I go to the country, take my fears and let go of them all.
I stand in the wilderness, looking across the valley and over
the slope.
There I feel peace, there I find hope.
Knowing all is well and that I'm going to cope.

I've cast away my fears,
And I shed no more tears.
After my journey I do come home and back through the door,
Free of my burden, and give love to others once more.

If WE Listen to our Media Peers

If you listen to your media peers
And allow them to coach and feed your fears,
And cause you to leave the safety of your home,
And the lonely streets to roam,
You'll wander on edge through your life each day,
As you've set yourself up for them as prey.

Soon you'll know you need a guide,
As you swallow your misplaced pride.
Then you ask, "Show me the direction I should go,
As the way back home, I seek to know."

I shall no longer listen to media peers,
Or allow them to shape my doubt or fears.
There's one who really cares for me,
As a reminder of Christ's love within the cross I see.

In the Caverns of your Mind

In the caverns of your mind
Treasured memories you may find.
Memories of a gentle touch,
That conveyed the love you shared so much.

Memories of a luscious kiss,
Soft and smooth just like wine; ho, what bliss.
Memories of a loving embrace,
As you touched face-to-face,
Hoping that this moment would forever last,
And wishing that time wouldn't go so fast.

In the caverns of your mind,
These may be the precious treasures that you find.
So when you are together, these memories tell
And remember those precious moments when in love you fell.

In the Midst of Youth

As a man in the midst of my youth,
I search for love, I search for truth.
My peers found love in their life,
And some got married and gained a wife.
For me, true love didn't come my way,
I felt rejected and alone for many a day.

My dream of a girl who, for me would love and care,
And with whom I, my life and love would share.
Hoping we'd grow strong in love as we journey in life,
And become as one, as man and wife.

Later in life my dream came true,
I found a lady who loved me too.
She was lovely, caring and so kind,
And as man and wife our hearts entwined.

So, my dream came true at last,
And my loneliness now was past.

Our love for many years did last, but sadly now my wife has passed away.
And I am alone again each day.
I really do miss her now she's not there.
I miss so much her love and care.
Will I ever again know such love,
And with such a gift be blessed by God above?

I Saw a Picture of a Man

I saw a picture of a man,
His head within his hands,
And on his face a look of doom.
And with a heart that was so full of gloom,
He said, "I feel the heartache and the pain."
And then he prays for some hope and peace to gain.
If he's your friend in despair,
Will you stay, and help, and care?

I Stand Upon an Open Beach

I stand upon an open beach
And see parents, the art of building castles their children
teach.
The children take a stick and write words within the sand.
Ho, it's such fun, they think it's really grand.

But sadly, the tide is coming in just now.
The children cry as the castle takes its final bow.
The words written upon the beach,
Washed away and out of reach.

How many castles have been built and words been written,
That over years by the rolling tides are smitten?
There's nothing left, for the tide washes it all away, you see,
Just like Christ's blood cleanses you and me.

I Take a Pebble

As I come into church, I take a pebble in my hand.
It seems slightly rough and not so grand,
But the dark spots that lay within
Now represent my shame and sin.

And as I go forth and place it in the bowl,
I feel the release within my soul.
And the dark spots begin to shine once more,
And I, to the Lord, make my heart and soul an open door.

Kind and Faithful

Faithfulness can be a faith in God within your heart, soul and
mind.
From which a deep sense of love and peace, you find.

Faithfulness can be the loyalty you show to family or friend.
When in their sadness, pain or loss to always be there, and to
their plight with compassion tend.

Being kind is showing courtesy and respect.
Whether in sickness or disability, you don't walk away and
them neglect.

Being kind is the care you give to the one you love.
Being kind is in the greeting that you give, whether it be,
"Good morning, love or guv."

If being kind and faithful is the way you live,
What a treasure from your heart, that with folks you share
and give.

Let my Life be a Song

I walk to church each Sunday morn,
As the birds sing their songs to greet the dawn.
I enter quietly into that holy place.
Gently within me the presence of the Holy Spirit trace.

I prepare myself to receive God's word
And hope the preacher can be heard.
And hear the message of today.
Then I continue to sing and pray.

And at the end of worship the blessing is given.
Now by God's word and Holy Spirit driven.
I seek to live out what I've just heard.
So let my life be a song that I sing out loud like a bird.

Life, a Journey

Life, a journey that we travel each day,
It just takes just one step to set us on our way.
Do we go left, or do we go right,
Into the dark, or into the light?

Do we follow greed, selfishness and a life full of shame,
And for all our faults, it's others we blame?
Or is kindness, compassion and loving care,
That from our hearts to all others we lovingly share?

Jesus says that we should love our neighbour,
So in our mission it should be at the heart of our labour.
If in your life all is dark, and nothing is right,
Please turn to Jesus and follow his light.

Lovely Dream

Last night a lovely dream I dreamed,
About a train that from a darkened tunnel steamed.
Aboard that train was my passion and my love,
She is, to me the world and above.

And as we arrived at the station,
We alighted at our destination.
On the platform I did before her kneel,
And expressed to her the love I feel.

I asked if she would marry me,
That together a life full of love and devotion see.
My heart now is full of joyfulness,
For my darling love has just said YES.

My Friend and I

My friend and I share each day,
We help and guide each other along the way.
He sees and I hear the beauty of the day;
He is deaf and I am blind,
And together the joy of nature find.

My friend tells me of the colours of the flowers, birds and
trees, but cannot hear their sound.
He speaks with passion of God's creation in the air and on the
ground.

I tell him of the sounds of birds that sing, as they perch upon
a branch or fly beneath a drifting cloud.
I explain that some sing soft and some sing very loud.

I tell him of the rustling leaves, as the air flows through the
trees.
I tell him what I hear, and he describes what he sees.

Together we accept each other,
As if we were brother to brother.
Disability does not mar the friendship that we found.
I ask, why can't it be the same for all in the world around?

My New Ministry

I take up my new church ministry now,
And before God and all you folks I make a promise and a
vow.
A promise to be there for the churches of the district day by
day;
A vow to guide you on the Christian way.

And share my ministry on sabbath days
As I, with you all, share in prayer and praise.
And as I deliver the written word,
I will speak loud and clear so that I can be heard.

This is the ministry I seek to give with Christian kindness,
care and love,
Guided by The Holy Word given by our Lord above.

On Mothering Sunday

On Mothering Sunday, we say thanks for our mother's love
and care.
And in our joy and pain for always being there.
Through our lives she helps us grow, and the rights and
wrongs of life to know.

A mother is there for her child, whether it is daughter or son.
Mother gave her baby love even before their life begun.
So, in thanks for our mother's love, we give thanks on this
special day.
And bring mum some flowers to express our love, and thank
you to mother say.

Pastoral Care

With pastoral ministry we give,
Into the journey of faith you live,
With support and prayers, we guide,
Seeking to be the Good Samaritan by your side.

In moments of stress or pain,
And its relief, peace or healing you seek to gain,
We come in fellowship by your side, praying together in the
Lord's presence, we abide.

And having found God's healing or inspiration,
We go forth to serve or minister to the Lord's congregation.
My time of ministry with you at this moment ends,
But with Christ I'm always there for you, my friends.

Paul

I have lived a life of bitterness and shame;
The hurt was mine, no one else could I blame.
I travel in my time with such a heavy load,
And as I travelled along the Damascus Road,
A light flashed before me and I fell to the ground.
As I got up, blinded, something new within my heart I
found.

Since that day, I write these letters to proclaim Christ's
teaching true.
These letters that are written in faith, I wrote for you.
And so, in this book is the path I trod,
A guide to help your journey of faith with God.

<u>Pretiumque et Causa Laboris me</u>

"Pretiumque et Causa Laboris me," you may,
At some point hear me say.
I'll tell you its meaning for you to savour,
For it says, "The prize and cause of my labour."
It is a theme that within me you may trace,
As each task I caringly embrace.

For it is you, my friends, who are the prize,
As I greet you with such joy within my eyes.
The love of friends is the treasure.
It causes me to rise each day, to give love and friendship back
to you, and to do it without measure.
The prize is the smile and words of friendship that you give;
The cause is the ring of love and friendship in which I seek to
live.

Now you know the meaning of this motto, please don't just let
it go or leave it on a shelf.
Embrace it with all your heart and live it for yourself.
Pretiumque et Causa Laboris me;
Let love and friendship become your prize, and the cause of
all you seek to be.

Rose Window

What light through yonder window breaks,
And from my mouth my breath it takes?
The beautiful, coloured images project upon the floor,
And as the sun sets, they slowly creep up to the door.

Each image tells the story of God's word,
That can be seen, if not heard.
'Tis a guide to the teachings of our God,
And to the paths that saints have trod.

This window within the cathedral is a rose,
A testimony to God's teachings pose.
A blessing to those who put it there,
And to those who stand and stare.
May it bless and touch their heart,
And in new-found faith God's mission start.

Seasons

Spring, it comes and melts away the winter snow.
Spring flowers blossom forth in colour and their beauty doth
show.
The trees, they change from winter red to spring green,
It's a most magical display to be seen.

The summer brings forth the lily and the rose.
Their fragrance excites your senses as you inhale through your
nose.
And in the farmers' field,
Rapeseed and wheat, A crop of food for us doth yield.

And we come to autumn, cold once more to know,
As the trees drop their seed again to sow,
The squirrels gather up the nuts all around,
And bury them somewhere in the ground.

The fingers of Jack Frost make things white all around,
And a jewel-like magic before our eyes is found.
It sparkles there in the sun,
To light the new day that has begun.

Winter comes with special days from yore,

And we shoot fireworks into the sky once more.

Then we dress our house and sing some Christmas songs,

And place the Christ child in a manger where he belongs.

A song of hope and joy we sing,

That hope, that joy into this New Year we seek to bring.

St Mary

St Mary, mother of a special child,
Who lays within her arms so gentle; he looks so meek and
mild.
St Mary held Christ gently to her breast.
Her beating heart burned strong with love for him within her
chest.

St Mary, the patron saint for mothers of today,
Is there for mums in parenthood to guide them on their way.
Take her presence to your heart,
And that burning love to your child impart.

St Michael and You

St Michael had such a battle with the evil one,
To conquer him, so sin and torment would be gone.
If you care to look around,
Such battles in life can still be found.

St Michael is still around today,
To help you conquer the devil's sinful prey.
Let him, today, cast his sword,
For it is formed from God's Holy Word.

St Michael will help you battle through the devil's evil crowd,
And cast away his evil shroud.
So you can dwell in peace with God,
And so to tread the path that saints have trod.

The Beauty of a Bird

The blackbird sings its song,
And I attempt to twitter along.
The song is so sweet,
I try to catch every tweet.
The wings glisten as they open to catch the breeze,
And the blackbird glides between the trees.

Then the woodpecker comes a-rapping
As upon the tree he's tapping.
His colours stand out so stark,
They even dazzle the morning lark.
Then a robin to my sight doth please,
So friendly is she, from my hand she eats my cheese.

And as the birds together, a beautiful chorus make,
And a place within God's choir take.
Within the woods that beautiful sound is heard.
That's the treasure of a bird.

The Beauty of a Winter's Day

I look out upon the snow
And once more, the blessing of this winter beauty know.
The snow glistens in the rising sun,
As this new day has just begun.

The trees stand so dark and bare,
And on each branch not a leaf is left hanging there.
The leaves lay piled upon the ground,
Giving rise to a rustling sound.
For as my friends I go to meet,
I like to kick the leaves with my feet.

The hedgerow, white with frost,
It replaces the greenery that's been lost.
The berries that hang there, o' so bright,
Make such a joyous winter sight.
The mistletoe hangs with such bliss,
Couples stop beneath, to steal a kiss.

Ho, what joy the winter gives
Amidst the cold its beauty lives.
The trees, hedgerows and the lawn
Shine so bright each frosty morn.
So treasure the beauty of each day,
For it so soon fades away.

The Face

As I look in the mirror and see the face from the past,
I see the face of youth I thought would always last.
The face of which, in love I fell,
And to you the words, "I love you," from its lips did tell.

The face of which you embraced and placed your face to mine,
Then you kissed me so soft and sweet like wine.
This face on which you put a smile and caused to express such glee,
Yes, that happened on the day you said you'd marry me.

I turn around to look at you and see,
Despite the lines upon my face you're still in love with me.
Although my face has wrinkly turned,
My love for you, my dearest, has never more brightly burned.

The Lord's Table

As we come before the Lord's table now,
We hold out our hands to receive and bow.
When the bread is placed into our palm,
A sense of peace we come to know,
This sustenance feeds our soul, and helps in wholeness so to
grow.

We take the wine and gently place it to our lip,
And savour every precious sip.
Its presence as the blood of Christ brings healing and
cleansing to our soul,
And now we feel completely whole.

And with the body and blood of Christ within, so blessed are
we when we walk back through the door,
And continue our journey of faith once more.

The Lonely Plate

A plate sits on the table all alone,
Fearing it would spend the festive season on its own.
But then the Brussel sprouts came out to dance,
And upon the plate's edge, they did prance.

The carrots came to join them too,
"We're so happy to be here, for it's so much better than the stew."
The pigs with blankets wrapped around,
Slid on the plate as their place they found.

Then the turkey came along, steaming hot,
Placed in the middle of the plate to be filled with sage and onion, was the only privilege that it got.

The mashed potatoes and the gravy came to complete this festive fayre.
The food said, "There's something missing, right just there."
The cranberry sauce came on late,
And spread its juice across the plate.

The plate said, "With all this food I'm not alone,
I won't face this festive season on my own."
So if you know someone that is all alone,
And to loneliness they are prone,

Share this season some festive fayre,
Show the kindness in your heart that they may know it comes
from there.

The Mercy Seat

There is a place within our church where we kneel, and within
our heart and soul we seek our Lord to greet.
That special place beneath the yellow, red and blue is called
The Mercy Seat.

'Tis the place that we come with our burden and our pain,
To seek his grace and by his gentle hand some healing hope to
gain.

We arise, and walk to the door, cleansed, healed by his
grace.
For as we knelt, within our mind we saw the love upon
Christ's face.

We arise and now march on with a mission given.
We step forth with confidence by the Holy Spirit, driven.
Give thanks for that special place where the Lord we can
meet.
That special place where we knelt that we call The Mercy
Seat.

There is Colour in this World

There is colour in this world that not all can see.
You see the yellow, red and green,
All we see is the dullness of the scene.

Some have, in all their days
Struggled to see life's colour ways.
CVD is not a joke,
But fun of them folks did poke.
You may a painter or electrician be,
But those opportunities are not there for folk who colours
cannot see.

If your friend suffers so,
Be kind and let them the colours know.
Show compassion and understand their disability,
And help them all the beauty of nature see.

There on that Dark Hill

There on that dark hill, where Christ died that we might live,
There was, planted within this world, the seed of love that
Christ to us did give.

A love with which the disciples lived and heard,
And recorded in God's Holy Word.
A love today by the Holy Spirit given,
And with that love within our heart, is a sense of mission
driven.

And so, with Christ-like love within our heart, and God's
Holy Spirit within our soul,
We march on in Christian faith, to spread that love and
achieve our mission's goal.

The Saints

The saints, they gather round us now,
As we in praise and confession bow,
And as we lift our praise unto the Lord,
The saints, they join in with every word.

The saints have shared this time of worship, yes, in every part.
And each saint with us felt the love of Christ within their heart.

And as we sing our final song of praise,
The saints with us, their voices raise.
And as we leave this conversation with the saints and God,
We go with clear vision, and follow the path the saints have trod.

The Steam Engine

The steam engine is such a majestic beast,
When in steam, to the eye is such a feast.
The pistons rock to and fro,
The wheels turn as off to its destination go.

Through the tunnels the engine goes at speed,
And at the other end emerges like a dragon freed.
You hear the sound of clickety clack
As it speeds along the track.

Then it rattles across the points
And returns to rhythm as it hits the joints.
The stoker, to make good time is his desire,
So he continues to shovel coal upon the fire.

The engine speeds as the hill goes down,
So the driver applies the brakes as the engine gets closer to the
town.
And so, the train stops at its destination,
Then folks alight onto the platform at the station.

Thursday Cake

Every Wednesday I make a delicious cake,
And on Thursday with it, a journey to the Hub Club I make.
I see the smiles upon their faces,
As their palettes the exciting flavour traces.

I make each cake with a heart full of kindness and
compassion,
And put it into the cake that I fashion.
I pour such love into the mixing bowl,
Not just a bit but the whole.

My saying is, "I love you to bits," a saying of mine you may
know,
A saying that deep in my heart it sits, and for you all
continues to grow.

Time of Silence Now

And now it's time to go to bed,
And for our prayers to be said,
And as we kneel at our chair,
We chatter on about family, our fears and joys just there.

But do we a time of silence take,
And allow time for the Lord, his message to make?
If we speak and chatter so,
How are we God's voice to know?
Make for yourself a silence vow,
And in the silence, listen to what God says just now.

Together in Friendship

Our walking group comes together on Tuesday each week.
We share in conversation, along with the joy and the
friendship we seek.

In this group there's Cath, Lyn, Pamela and Sue, all lovely
lasses, to mention a few;
Tony, John, Graham and Chris are some of the guys that
come along too.

Together in friendship we laugh and we talk,
As around Brocks Hill Country Park the miles we walk.
At the end of the walk, I go to the café
And, with Tony, John, Graham, Chris and others like
Pamela, Lyn, Sue and Cath,
To share in the friendship and chatter and have a good laugh.

Trinket Box

As I take this trinket box from the drawer,
I think of past loves and friendships from before.
As I touch each brooch and ring,
Fond memories of past romances it doth bring.
The rings that lay within my palms,
Were given to me as he held me in his arms.

But today we're together once again,
For being apart caused such pain.
Now together we made a vow,
The future's bright, for we are married now.

The rings, that in the trinket box for a time did linger,
Are now securely sparkling on my finger.
Don't be quick to cast romance into a trinket box,
But be ready to open your heart's door when true love upon it
knocks.

Walking in the Rain

As we go walking in the rain,
Some folks think that we're insane.
But as we journey along together,
It doesn't matter about the weather.

It is friendship we come to share.
Amidst our group there is kindness and compassion, as for
each other we show our care.

And so, despite the pouring rain,
We sit and have a coffee and share our joy and pain.
And as we from the group depart,
There is a joy within our heart,
For the friendship we have made,
It is the treasure we will not trade.

Walk Through Pastures Green

As I walk through pastures green
And survey the beauty of the scene,
And look upon the still waters of the lake,
I linger and a slower step I take.
I smell the sweetness of the air I breathe.
It brings such joy use and my stress relieve.

My trusty staff supports me still.
As I climb the hill
Before me now,
It helps me on my journey to the brow.
And as I reach the top, with my eyes wide open and my
mouth open wide,
I gaze at the beauty on the other side.

This journey is a joy to me,
As I, the beauty of God's creation see.
He has blessed me on this day.
My thanks to him I give and pray,
That other folks be blessed this way.

What Beauty

What is this that before me grows,
And to the world its beauty shows?
Its arms reach out and up to the sky
And offers shelter to passers-by.

Offers shade from the sun,
And shelter when the rains begun.
From the gentle rustle of the leaves,
Our heart and mind, a sense of calm and peace receives.

'Tis a tree that I speak of,
A gift from God, a gift of love.
Just like the tree,
God shelters you and me,
So that through our lives his beauty see.

When Mending my Shed

When mending my shed, I grazed my leg upon the door.
I was in pain and the blood began to pour.
I cried and shouted, and sought the help of my neighbour,
who's a nurse, you see.
She came so kindly, and gently she tended my wound for me.

No longer was I blooded or pained.
By her skill, relief I gained.
And so, it is through the mending of a shed,
I am free of the loneliness I dread.
Although my pain is at an end,
I have found a precious friend.

Whistling Sound

The wind, it blows through the trees,
And blows away the fallen leaves.
The wind doth sweep across the ground,
And comes along with its whistling sound.

It rattles the windows and shakes the doors,
And sweeps across the open moors;
And sweeps away all that's loose on the ground,
And sings its song with a whistling sound.

Now it's quiet and we have some peace,
The wind is going, and the whistle does cease.
But one thing that we know for sure,
The wind will be back and whistle once more.

ABOUT THE AUTHOR

Let me introduce myself, I'm Michael J Gardner Aka The Walking Poet. Why the Walking Poet you ask. Well I am a volunteer wellbeing walk leader for my local borough council. But when I started with the group I was prescribed to it by a Social Prescriptive Link Worker after my wife died. The group was the best place for me, they helped a lot.

When I was working I was a safety rep, and when I was mid sixty's I trained as a Lay Preacher, my poems are written in the way they are because I write what I feel. And writing that way these poems I share with you have been a good therapy to get me through my grief. I am now a Volunteer for Leicestershire, Leicester and Rutland Headway.

Michael's Other Book

www.green-cat.shop/michael-j-gardner

For more information about our books and services

Please visit

www.green-cat.shop

Printed in Great Britain
by Amazon

43924565R00040